HAL•LEONARD
INSTRUMENTAL
PLAY-ALONG

FLUTE

AUDIO ACCESS INCLUDED

PLAYBACK+
Speed • Pitch • Balance • Loop

Billie Eilish

T0087305

Audio arrangements by Peter Deneff

To access audio, visit:
www.halleonard.com/mylibrary

"Enter Code"
1445-2341-1238-7442

ISBN 978-1-5400-9207-6

HAL•LEONARD®

Visit Hal Leonard Online at
www.halleonard.com

Contact us:
Hal Leonard
7777 West Bluemound Road
Milwaukee, WI 53213
Email: info@halleonard.com

In Europe, contact:
Hal Leonard Europe Limited
42 Wigmore Street
Marylebone, London, W1U 2RN
Email: info@halleonardeurope.com

In Australia, contact:
Hal Leonard Australia Pty. Ltd.
4 Lentara Court
Cheltenham, Victoria, 3192 Australia
Email: info@halleonard.com.au

CONTENTS

BAD GUY

FLUTE

Words and Music by BILLIE EILISH O'CONNELL
and FINNEAS O'CONNELL

I LOVE YOU

FLUTE

Words and Music by BILLIE EILISH O'CONNELL
and FINNEAS O'CONNELL

Idontwannabeyouanymore

FLUTE

Words and Music by BILLIE EILISH O'CONNELL
and FINNEAS O'CONNELL

LOVELY

FLUTE

Words and Music by BILLIE EILISH O'CONNELL,
FINNEAS O'CONNELL and KHALID ROBINSON

NO TIME TO DIE

FLUTE

Words and Music by BILLIE EILISH O'CONNELL
and FINNEAS O'CONNELL

Slowly, mysteriously

3
f
p

OCEAN EYES

FLUTE

Words and Music by
FINNEAS O'CONNELL

1.
2.
mp

YOU SHOULD SEE ME IN A CROWN

FLUTE

Words and Music by BILLIE EILISH O'CONNELL
and FINNEAS O'CONNELL

D.S. al Coda
CODA
mf
2
mf
f
1.
2.

WHEN THE PARTY'S OVER

FLUTE

Words and Music by
FINNEAS O'CONNELL